FORWARD/COMMENTARY

The National Institute of Standards and Technology (NIST) is a measurement standards laboratory, and a non-regulatory agency of the United States Department of Commerce. Its mission is to promote innovation and industrial competitiveness. Founded in 1901, as the National Bureau of Standards, NIST was formed with the mandate to provide standard weights and measures, and to serve as the national physical laboratory for the United States. With a world-class measurement and testing laboratory encompassing a wide range of areas of computer science, mathematics, statistics, and systems engineering, NIST's cybersecurity program supports its overall mission to promote U.S. innovation and industrial competitiveness by advancing measurement science, standards, and related technology through research and development in ways that enhance economic security and improve our quality of life.

The need for cybersecurity standards and best practices that address interoperability, usability and privacy has been shown to be critical for the nation. NIST's cybersecurity programs seek to enable greater development and application of practical, innovative security technologies and methodologies that enhance the country's ability to address current and future computer and information security challenges.

The cybersecurity publications produced by NIST cover a wide range of cybersecurity concepts that are carefully designed to work together to produce a holistic approach to cybersecurity primarily for government agencies and constitute the best practices used by industry. This holistic strategy to cybersecurity covers the gamut of security subjects from development of secure encryption standards for communication and storage of information while at rest to how best to recover from a cyber-attack.

The field of computer science is rapidly changing from the basic personal computer to the "Internet of Things". Many of these devices were not designed to be "connected" and very little thought was given to secure them from cyber-attack. Recent events have clearly demonstrated the need to secure everything from web cams to electrical utility grids.

That's where NIST comes in. Just as the National Bureau of Standards set the standard for weights and measures at the beginning of the last century, the 21st century mission for NIST is to set the standard for cybersecurity. NIST gathers the very best minds in industry and government and serves as the central clearing house for information that sets the standard for security for the nation. This publication is only one piece in the mosaic of publications NIST produces but each is a vital key in its own field to the overall cybersecurity strategy that government and industry must adopt in the public interest. All NIST publications are freely available for download over the internet to maximize adoption of the standards.

This NIST Special Publication is an integral part of the overall design, development and maintenance of an IT security infrastructure that ensures confidentiality, integrity, and availability of mission critical information. It was developed to assist in choosing IT security products that meet an organization's requirements. It should be used with other NIST publications to develop a comprehensive approach to managing, satisfying, and verifying an organization's IT security and information assurance requirements.

We here at 4th Watch Books are former government employees so we know how government employees actually use the standards. When a new standard is released, an engineer prints it out, punches holes and puts it in a 3-ring binder. While this is not a big deal for a 5 or 10-page document, many NIST documents are over 100 pages and printing a large document is a time-consuming effort. Unfortunately, reductions in government over the years means that now the engineer himself has to print his own copy (no one has a secretary anymore). So, an engineer that's paid $75 an hour is spending hours simply printing out the tools he needs to do his job. That's time that could be better spent doing engineering.

4th Watch Books prints these documents so engineers can focus on what they were hired to do – engineering. This is important because there are not as many engineers working in government as there used to be, so wasted time on clerical duties is unproductive. As a former senior leader in the government, I always encouraged my subordinates to look for ways to do things better, faster, cheaper. I always asked my staff to focus on the objective and consider the cost/benefit analysis of everything they do. If something can be done better, faster and cheaper, then we would be remiss if we didn't take advantage of the opportunity.

This book is a perfect example of that type of thinking. Rather than spend the limited resources we have at a particular agency to develop cybersecurity solutions, it will always be better, faster and cheaper to embrace a standard that has been fully-developed and totally integrated in the wider scheme of things by the engineers at NIST with the help they receive from industry.

Luis Ayala
Writer and Publisher, 4th Watch Books

NIST Special Publication 800-150

Guide to Cyber Threat Information Sharing

Chris Johnson
Lee Badger
David Waltermire
Julie Snyder
Clem Skorupka

This publication is available free of charge from:
http://dx.doi.org/10.6028/NIST.SP.800-150

COMPUTER SECURITY

NIST Special Publication 800-150

Guide to Cyber Threat Information Sharing

Chris Johnson
Lee Badger
David Waltermire
Computer Security Division
Information Technology Laboratory

Julie Snyder
Clem Skorupka
The MITRE Corporation

This publication is available free of charge from:
http://dx.doi.org/10.6028/NIST.SP.800-150

October 2016

U.S. Department of Commerce
Penny Pritzker, Secretary

National Institute of Standards and Technology
Willie May, Under Secretary of Commerce for Standards and Technology and Director

Authority

This publication has been developed by NIST in accordance with its statutory responsibilities under the Federal Information Security Modernization Act (FISMA) of 2014, 44 U.S.C. § 3551 *et seq.*, Public Law (P.L.) 113-283. NIST is responsible for developing information security standards and guidelines, including minimum requirements for federal information systems, but such standards and guidelines shall not apply to national security systems without the express approval of appropriate federal officials exercising policy authority over such systems. This guideline is consistent with the requirements of the Office of Management and Budget (OMB) Circular A-130.

Nothing in this publication should be taken to contradict the standards and guidelines made mandatory and binding on federal agencies by the Secretary of Commerce under statutory authority. Nor should these guidelines be interpreted as altering or superseding the existing authorities of the Secretary of Commerce, Director of the OMB, or any other federal official. This publication may be used by nongovernmental organizations on a voluntary basis and is not subject to copyright in the United States. Attribution would, however, be appreciated by NIST.

National Institute of Standards and Technology Special Publication 800-150
Natl. Inst. Stand. Technol. Spec. Publ. 800-150, 35 pages (October 2016)
CODEN: NSPUE2

This publication is available free of charge from:
http://dx.doi.org/10.6028/NIST.SP.800-150

Certain commercial entities, equipment, or materials may be identified in this document in order to describe an experimental procedure or concept adequately. Such identification is not intended to imply recommendation or endorsement by NIST, nor is it intended to imply that the entities, materials, or equipment are necessarily the best available for the purpose.

There may be references in this publication to other publications currently under development by NIST in accordance with its assigned statutory responsibilities. The information in this publication, including concepts and methodologies, may be used by federal agencies even before the completion of such companion publications. Thus, until each publication is completed, current requirements, guidelines, and procedures, where they exist, remain operative. For planning and transition purposes, federal agencies may wish to closely follow the development of these new publications by NIST.

Organizations are encouraged to review all draft publications during public comment periods and provide feedback to NIST. Many NIST cybersecurity publications, other than the ones noted above, are available at http://csrc.nist.gov/publications.

Comments on this publication may be submitted to:

National Institute of Standards and Technology
Attn: Computer Security Division, Information Technology Laboratory
100 Bureau Drive (Mail Stop 8930) Gaithersburg, MD 20899-8930
Email: sp800-150comments@nist.gov

All comments are subject to release under the Freedom of Information Act (FOIA).

Reports on Computer Systems Technology

The Information Technology Laboratory (ITL) at the National Institute of Standards and Technology (NIST) promotes the U.S. economy and public welfare by providing technical leadership for the Nation's measurement and standards infrastructure. ITL develops tests, test methods, reference data, proof of concept implementations, and technical analyses to advance the development and productive use of information technology. ITL's responsibilities include the development of management, administrative, technical, and physical standards and guidelines for the cost-effective security and privacy of other than national security-related information in federal information systems. The Special Publication 800-series reports on ITL's research, guidelines, and outreach efforts in information system security, and its collaborative activities with industry, government, and academic organizations.

Abstract

Cyber threat information is any information that can help an organization identify, assess, monitor, and respond to cyber threats. Cyber threat information includes indicators of compromise; tactics, techniques, and procedures used by threat actors; suggested actions to detect, contain, or prevent attacks; and the findings from the analyses of incidents. Organizations that share cyber threat information can improve their own security postures as well as those of other organizations.

This publication provides guidelines for establishing and participating in cyber threat information sharing relationships. This guidance helps organizations establish information sharing goals, identify cyber threat information sources, scope information sharing activities, develop rules that control the publication and distribution of threat information, engage with existing sharing communities, and make effective use of threat information in support of the organization's overall cybersecurity practices.

Keywords

cyber threat; cyber threat information sharing; indicators; information security; information sharing

Acknowledgments

The authors, Chris Johnson, Lee Badger, and David Waltermire of the National Institute of Standards and Technology (NIST), and Julie Snyder and Clem Skorupka of The MITRE Corporation, wish to thank their colleagues who contributed to this publication, including Tom Millar and Rich Struse of the Department of Homeland Security (DHS); Karen Quigg, Richard Murad, Carlos Blazquez, and Jon Baker of The MITRE Corporation; Murugiah Souppaya and Melanie Cook of NIST; Ryan Meeuf, of the Software Engineering Institute, Carnegie Mellon University; George Saylor, Greg Witte, and Matt Smith of G2 Inc.; Karen Scarfone of Scarfone Cybersecurity; Chris Bean of the National Security Agency (NSA); Eric Burger of the Georgetown Center for Secure Communications, Georgetown University; Joe Drissel of Cyber Engineering Services Inc.; Tony Sager of the Center for Internet Security; Kent Landfield of Intel Security; Bruce Potter of KEYW Inc.; Jeff Carpenter of Dell SecureWorks; Ben Miller of the North American Electric Reliability Corporation (NERC); Anton Chuvakin of Gartner, Inc.; Johannes Ullrich of the SANS Technology Institute; Patrick Dempsey, Defense Industrial Base Collaborative Information Sharing Environment (DCISE); Matthew Schuster, Mass Insight; Garrett Schubert of EMC; James Caulfield of the Federal Reserve; Bob Guay of Biogen; and Chris Sullivan of Courion.

Trademark Information

All registered trademarks or trademarks belong to their respective organizations.

Executive Summary

Cyber attacks have increased in frequency and sophistication, presenting significant challenges for organizations that must defend their data and systems from capable threat actors. These actors range from individual, autonomous attackers to well-resourced groups operating in a coordinated manner as part of a criminal enterprise or on behalf of a nation-state. Threat actors can be persistent, motivated, and agile, and they use a variety of tactics, techniques, and procedures (TTPs) to compromise systems, disrupt services, commit financial fraud, and expose or steal intellectual property and other sensitive information. Given the risks these threats present, it is increasingly important that organizations share cyber threat information and use it to improve their security posture.

Cyber threat information is any information that can help an organization identify, assess, monitor, and respond to cyber threats. Examples of cyber threat information include indicators (system artifacts or observables associated with an attack), TTPs, security alerts, threat intelligence reports, and recommended security tool configurations. Most organizations already produce multiple types of cyber threat information that are available to share internally as part of their information technology and security operations efforts.

By exchanging cyber threat information within a sharing community, organizations can leverage the collective knowledge, experience, and capabilities of that sharing community to gain a more complete understanding of the threats the organization may face. Using this knowledge, an organization can make threat-informed decisions regarding defensive capabilities, threat detection techniques, and mitigation strategies. By correlating and analyzing cyber threat information from multiple sources, an organization can also enrich existing information and make it more actionable. This enrichment may be achieved by independently confirming the observations of other community members, and by improving the overall quality of the threat information through the reduction of ambiguity and errors. Organizations that receive threat information and subsequently use this information to remediate a threat confer a degree of protection to other organizations by impeding the threat's ability to spread. Additionally, sharing of cyber threat information allows organizations to better detect campaigns that target particular industry sectors, business entities, or institutions.

This publication assists organizations in establishing and participating in cyber threat information sharing relationships. The publication describes the benefits and challenges of sharing, clarifies the importance of trust, and introduces specific data handling considerations. The goal of the publication is to provide guidelines that improve cybersecurity operations and risk management activities through safe and effective information sharing practices, and that help organizations plan, implement, and maintain information sharing.

NIST encourages greater sharing of cyber threat information among organizations, both in acquiring threat information from other organizations and in providing internally-generated threat information to other organizations. Implementing the following recommendations enables organizations to make more efficient and effective use of information sharing capabilities.

Establish information sharing goals and objectives that support business processes and security policies.

An organization's information sharing goals and objectives should advance its overall cybersecurity strategy and help an organization more effectively manage cyber-related risk. An organization should use the combined knowledge and experience of its own personnel and others, such as members of cyber threat information sharing organizations, to share threat information while operating per its security, privacy, regulatory, and legal compliance requirements.

Identify existing internal sources of cyber threat information.

Organizations should identify tools, sensors, and repositories that collect, produce, or store cyber threat information, threat analytics platforms, and delivery mechanisms that support the exchange of cyber threat information. As internal cyber threat information sources and capabilities are identified, organizations should determine how information from these sources currently support cybersecurity and risk management activities. Organizations should also document observed knowledge gaps and consider acquiring additional threat information from other (possibly external) sources or through the deployment of other tools or sensors. Finally, organizations should identify threat information that is available and suitable for sharing with outside parties.

Specify the scope of information sharing activities.

The breadth of an organization's information sharing activities should be consistent with its resources, abilities, and objectives. Information sharing efforts should focus on activities that provide the greatest value to an organization and its sharing partners. The scoping activity should identify types of information that an organization's key stakeholders authorize for sharing, the circumstances under which sharing of this information is permitted, and those with whom the information can and should be shared.

Establish information sharing rules.

Sharing rules are intended to control the publication and distribution of threat information, and consequently help to prevent the dissemination of information that, if improperly disclosed, may have adverse consequences for an organization, its customers, or its business partners. Information sharing rules should take into consideration the trustworthiness of the recipient, the sensitivity of the shared information, and the potential impact of sharing (or not sharing) specific types of information.

Join and participate in information sharing efforts.

An organization should identify and participate in sharing activities that complement its existing threat information capabilities. An organization may need to participate in multiple information sharing forums to meet its operational needs. Organizations should consider public and private sharing communities, government repositories, commercial cyber threat information feeds, and open sources such as public websites, blogs, and data feeds.

Actively seek to enrich indicators by providing additional context, corrections, or suggested improvements.

When possible, organizations should increase the usefulness and effectiveness of threat information by producing metadata for each indicator that is generated. Such metadata can provide context regarding the indicator by describing the intended use of the indicator, how it is to be interpreted, and how it relates to other indicators. Additionally, sharing processes should include mechanisms for publishing indicators, updating indicators and associated metadata, and retracting submissions that are incorrect or perhaps inadvertently shared. Such feedback plays an important role in the enrichment, maturation, and quality of the indicators shared within a community.

Use secure, automated workflows to publish, consume, analyze, and act upon cyber threat information.

The use of standardized data formats and transport protocols to share cyber threat information makes it easier to automate threat information processing. The use of automation enables cyber threat information to be rapidly shared, transformed, enriched, analyzed, and acted upon with less need for manual intervention.

Proactively establish cyber threat sharing agreements.

Rather than attempting to establish sharing agreements during an active cyber incident, organizations should plan ahead and have agreements in place before incidents occur. Such advanced planning helps ensure that participating organizations establish trusted relationships and understand their roles, responsibilities, and information handling requirements.

Protect the security and privacy of sensitive information.

Sensitive information such as controlled unclassified information (CUI) [16] and personally identifiable information (PII) may be encountered when handling cyber threat information. The improper disclosure of such information could cause financial loss; violate laws, regulations, and contracts; be cause for legal action; or damage an organization's or individual's reputation. Accordingly, organizations should implement the necessary security and privacy controls and handling procedures to protect this information from unauthorized disclosure or modification.

Provide ongoing support for information sharing activities.

Each organization should establish an information sharing plan that provides for ongoing infrastructure maintenance and user support. The plan should address the collection and analysis of threat information from both internal and external sources and the use of this information in the development and deployment of protective measures. A sustainable approach is necessary to ensure that resources are available for the ongoing collection, storage, analysis, and dissemination of cyber threat information.

Table of Contents

List of Appendices

List of Tables

1. Introduction

1.1 Purpose and Scope

This publication provides guidance to help organizations exchange cyber threat information. The guidance addresses sharing of cyber threat information within an organization, consuming and using cyber threat information received from external sources, and producing cyber threat information that can be shared with other organizations. The document also presents specific considerations for participation in information sharing communities.

This publication expands upon the information sharing concepts introduced in Section 4, Coordination and Information Sharing, of NIST Special Publication (SP) 800-61[1].

1.2 Audience

This publication is intended for computer security incident response teams (CSIRTs), system and network administrators, cybersecurity specialists, privacy officers, technical support staff, chief information security officers (CISOs), chief information officers (CIOs), computer security program managers, and others who are key stakeholders in cyber threat information sharing activities.

Although this guidance is written primarily for federal agencies, it is intended to be applicable to a wide variety of governmental and non-governmental organizations.

1.3 Document Structure

The remainder of this document is organized into the following sections and appendices:

- **Section 2** introduces basic cyber threat information sharing concepts, describes the benefits of sharing information, and discusses the challenges faced by organizations as they implement sharing capabilities.

- **Section 3** provides guidelines on establishing sharing relationships with other organizations.

- **Section 4** discusses considerations for effectively participating in sharing relationships.

- **Appendix A** contains scenarios that show how organizations can enhance their network defenses by sharing cyber threat information and by leveraging the cyber experience and capabilities of their partners.

- **Appendix B** contains a list of terms used in the document and their associated definitions.

- **Appendix C** provides a list of acronyms used in the document.

- **Appendix D** identifies resources referenced in the document.

2.   Basics of Cyber Threat Information Sharing

This section introduces basic cyber threat information sharing concepts including types of cyber threat information and common terminology. The section also examines potential uses for shared cyber threat information and explores the benefits and challenges of threat information sharing.

2.1   Threat Information Types

A *cyber threat* is "any circumstance or event with the potential to adversely impact organizational operations (including mission, functions, image, or reputation), organizational assets, individuals, other organizations, or the Nation through an information system via unauthorized access, destruction, disclosure, or modification of information, and/or denial of service." [2] For brevity, this publication uses the term *threat* instead of "cyber threat". The individuals and groups posing threats are known as "threat actors" or simply *actors*.

Threat information is any information related to a threat that might help an organization protect itself against a threat or detect the activities of an actor. Major types of threat information include the following:

- *Indicators* are technical artifacts or observables[1] that suggest an attack is imminent or is currently underway or that a compromise may have already occurred. Indicators can be used to detect and defend against potential threats. Examples of indicators include the Internet Protocol (IP) address of a suspected command and control server, a suspicious Domain Name System (DNS) domain name, a Uniform Resource Locator (URL) that references malicious content, a file hash for a malicious executable, or the subject line text of a malicious email message.

- *Tactics, techniques, and procedures (TTPs)* describe the behavior of an actor. *Tactics* are high-level descriptions of behavior, *techniques* are detailed descriptions of behavior in the context of a tactic, and *procedures* are even lower-level, highly detailed descriptions in the context of a technique. TTPs could describe an actor's tendency to use a specific malware variant, order of operations, attack tool, delivery mechanism (e.g., phishing or watering hole attack), or exploit.

- *Security alerts,* also known as advisories, bulletins, and vulnerability notes, are brief, usually human-readable, technical notifications regarding current vulnerabilities, exploits, and other security issues. Security alerts originate from sources such as the United States Computer Emergency Readiness Team (US-CERT), Information Sharing and Analysis Centers (ISACs), the National Vulnerability Database (NVD), Product Security Incident Response Teams (PSIRTs), commercial security service providers, and security researchers.

- *Threat intelligence reports* are generally prose documents that describe TTPs, actors, types of systems and information being targeted, and other threat-related information that provides greater situational awareness to an organization. Threat intelligence is threat information that has been aggregated, transformed, analyzed, interpreted, or enriched to provide the necessary context for decision-making processes.

- *Tool configurations* are recommendations for setting up and using tools (mechanisms) that support the automated collection, exchange, processing, analysis, and use of threat information. For example, tool configuration information could consist of instructions on how to install and use a rootkit

---

[1] An *observable* is an event (benign or malicious) on a network or system.

detection and removal utility, or how to create and customize intrusion detection signatures, router access control lists (ACLs), firewall rules, or web filter configuration files.

Many organizations already produce and share threat information internally. For example, an organization's security team may identify malicious files on a compromised system when responding to an incident and produce an associated set of indicators (e.g., file names, sizes, hash values). These indicators might then be shared with system administrators who configure security tools, such as host-based intrusion detection systems, to detect the presence of these indicators on other systems. Likewise, the security team may launch an email security awareness initiative in response to an observed rise in phishing attacks within the organization. These practices demonstrate information sharing within an organization.

The primary goal of this publication is to foster similar threat information sharing practices across organizational boundaries – both acquiring threat information from other organizations, and providing internally-generated threat information to other organizations.

2.2   Benefits of Information Sharing

Threat information sharing provides access to threat information that might otherwise be unavailable to an organization. Using shared resources, organizations can enhance their security posture by leveraging the knowledge, experience, and capabilities of their partners in a proactive way. Allowing "one organization's detection to become another's prevention"[2] is a powerful paradigm that can advance the overall security of organizations that actively share threat information.

An organization can use shared threat information in many ways. Some uses are operationally oriented, such as updating enterprise security controls for continuous monitoring with new indicators and configurations to detect the latest attacks and compromises. Threat information may also be used strategically, such as using shared threat information as inputs when planning major changes to an organization's security architecture.

Threat information exchanged within communities organized around specific industries or sectors (or some other shared characteristic) can be particularly beneficial because the member organizations often face actors that use common TTPs that target the same types of systems and information. Cyber defense is most effective when organizations work together to deter and defend against well-organized, capable actors. Such collaboration helps to reduce risk and improve the organization's security posture.

Benefits of information sharing include:

- **Shared Situational Awareness.** Information sharing enables organizations to leverage the collective knowledge, experience, and analytic capabilities of their sharing partners within a community of interest, thereby enhancing the defensive capabilities of multiple organizations. Even a single contribution—a new indicator or observation about an actor—can increase the awareness and security of an entire community.

- **Improved Security Posture.** By developing and sharing threat information, organizations gain a better understanding of the threat environment and can use threat information to inform their cybersecurity and risk management practices. Using shared information, organizations can identify affected platforms or systems, implement protective measures, enhance detection capabilities, and more effectively respond and recover from incidents based on observed changes in the threat environment. As organizations share information and subsequently mitigate threats, those

---

[2] This phrase, which has been used in numerous presentations and discussions, was formulated by Tony Sager, Senior VP and Chief Evangelist, Center for Internet Security.

organizations can improve their overall cybersecurity posture, even providing a degree of protection to other organizations, including those who may not have responded to the threat information, by reducing the number of viable attack vectors for actors.

- **Knowledge Maturation.** When seemingly unrelated observations are shared and analyzed by organizations, those observations can be correlated with data collected by others. This enrichment process increases the value of information by enhancing existing indicators and by developing knowledge of actor TTPs that are associated with a specific incident, threat, or threat campaign. Correlation can also impart valuable insights into the relationships that exist between indicators.

- **Greater Defensive Agility.** Actors continually adapt their TTPs to try to evade detection, circumvent security controls, and exploit new vulnerabilities. Organizations that share information are often better informed about changing TTPs and the need to rapidly detect and respond to threats. This awareness helps increase their operational tempo and reduce the probability of successful attack. Such agility also creates economies of scale for network defenders while increasing actors' costs by forcing them to develop new TTPs.

2.3   Challenges to Information Sharing

While sharing threat information clearly has benefits, certain challenges still remain. Some challenges that apply both to consuming and to producing threat information are:

- **Establishing Trust.** Trust relationships form the basis for information sharing, but require effort to establish and maintain. Ongoing communication through regular in-person meetings, phone calls, or social media can help accelerate the process of building trust.

- **Achieving Interoperability and Automation**. Standardized data formats and transport protocols are important building blocks for interoperability. The use of common formats and protocols enables automation and allows organizations, repositories, and tools to exchange threat information at machine speed. Adopting specific formats and protocols, however, can require significant time and resources, and the value of these investments can be substantially reduced if sharing partners require different formats or protocols. During the standards development process, early adopters need to accept the risk that it may be necessary to purchase new tools if significant changes to formats and protocols take place.

- **Safeguarding Sensitive Information**. Disclosure of sensitive information, such as controlled unclassified information (CUI) and personally identifiable information (PII) can result in financial loss, violation of sharing agreements, legal action, and loss of reputation. Sharing security and event information, such as security logs or scan results, could expose the protective or detective capabilities of the organization and result in threat shifting by the actor.[3] The unauthorized disclosure of information may impede or disrupt an ongoing investigation, jeopardize information needed for future legal proceedings, or disrupt response actions such as botnet takedown operations. Organizations should apply handling designations to shared information and implement policies, procedures, and technical controls to actively manage the risks of disclosure of sensitive information.

---

[3] NIST SP 800-30 Revision 1, *Guide for Conducting Risk Assessments*, defines threat shifting as "the response of adversaries to perceived safeguards and/or countermeasures (i.e., security controls), in which adversaries change some characteristic of their intent/targeting in order to avoid and/or overcome those safeguards/countermeasures. Threat shifting can occur in one or more domains including: (i) the time domain (e.g., a delay in an attack or illegal entry to conduct additional surveillance); (ii) the target domain (e.g., selecting a different target that is not as well protected); (iii) the resource domain (e.g., adding resources to the attack in order to reduce uncertainty or overcome safeguards and/or countermeasures); or (iv) the attack planning/attack method domain (e.g., changing the attack weapon or attack path)." [2, p.9]

- **Protecting Classified Information.** Information received from government sources may be marked as classified, making it difficult for an organization to use. Acquiring and maintaining the clearances needed for ongoing access to classified information sources is expensive and time-consuming for organizations. In addition, many organizations employ non-U.S. citizens who are not eligible to hold security clearances and are not permitted access to classified information. [3]

- **Enabling Information Consumption and Publication**. Organizations that want to consume and publish threat information need to have the necessary infrastructure, tools, personnel, and training to do so. Information sharing initiatives should be carefully scoped, because high-frequency, high-volume information exchanges have the potential to overwhelm an organization's processing capabilities. Organizations that are currently unable to support automated indicator exchange can explore other options such as the manual exchange of best practices or summary indicator information. As additional resources become available, an organization may decide to use automated tools and workflows to process and use threat information.

Some information sharing challenges apply only to the consumption of threat information:

- **Accessing External Information**. Organizations need the infrastructure to access external sources and incorporate the information retrieved from external sources into local decision-making processes. Information received from external sources has value only to the extent that an organization is equipped to act on the information.

- **Evaluating the Quality of Received Information**. Before acting on threat information, an organization needs to confirm that the information is correct, that the threat is relevant, and that the risks of using or not using the information (i.e., potential impacts of action vs. inaction) are well understood.

Several challenges are only applicable if an organization wants to provide its own information to other organizations:

- **Complying with Legal and Organizational Requirements.** An organization's executive and legal teams may restrict the types of information that the organization can provide to others. Such restrictions may include limits on the types of information and the level of technical detail provided. These safeguards are appropriate when they address legitimate business, legal, or privacy concerns, but the imposition of unwarranted or arbitrary restrictions may diminish the utility, availability, quality, and timeliness of shared information.

- **Limiting Attribution.** Organizations may openly participate in information sharing communities, but still require that their contributions remain anonymous. Unattributed information sharing may allow an organization to share more information because there is less perceived risk to the organization's reputation. The lack of attribution may, however, limit the usefulness of the information because users may have less confidence in information that originates from an unknown source. If the original sources of information cannot be identified, organizations may be unable to confirm that information has been received from multiple independent sources, and thus reduce an organization's ability to build confidence in received information.

3.   Establishing Sharing Relationships

When launching a threat information sharing capability, the following planning and preparation activities are recommended:[4]

- Define the goals and objectives of information sharing (section 3.1).

- Identify internal sources of threat information (section 3.2).

- Define the scope of information sharing activities (section 3.3).

- Establish information sharing rules (section 3.4).

- Join a sharing community (section 3.5).

- Plan to provide ongoing support for information sharing activities (section 3.6).

Throughout this process, organizations are encouraged to consult with subject matter experts both inside and outside their organization. Such sources include:

- Experienced cybersecurity personnel,

- Members and operators of established threat information sharing organizations,

- Trusted business associates, supply chain partners, and industry peers, and

- Personnel knowledgeable about legal issues, internal business processes, procedures, and systems.

An organization should use the knowledge and experience from these experts to help shape a threat information sharing capability that supports its mission and operates under its security, privacy, regulatory, and legal compliance requirements. Due to constantly changing risks, requirements, priorities, technology, and/or regulations, this process will often be iterative. Organizations should reassess and adjust their information sharing capabilities as needed based on changing circumstances. Such a change may involve repeating some or all of the planning and preparation activities listed above.

3.1   Define Information Sharing Goals and Objectives

At the outset, an organization should establish goals and objectives that describe the desired outcomes of threat information sharing in terms of the organization's business processes and security policies. These goals and objectives will help guide the organization through the process of scoping its information sharing efforts, selecting and joining sharing communities, and providing ongoing support for information sharing activities. Due to technological and/or resource constraints, it may be necessary to prioritize goals and objectives to ensure that the most important information sharing activities are performed.

3.2   Identify Internal Sources of Cyber Threat Information

A key step in any information sharing effort is to identify potential sources of threat information within an organization. By conducting an inventory of internal threat information sources, an organization is better able to identify knowledge gaps. These gaps can be addressed by deploying additional tools and sensors or by acquiring threat information from external threat information feeds or repositories. In large

---

[4] Although an order for these activities is described, in practice the sequence of these activities can vary, and activities can even be performed concurrently. For example, when joining an established sharing organization, it may make sense to address information sharing rules as part of joining the community.

organizations, this inventory process is also a means of discovering information that is being collected and analyzed in business units across the organization that may not be currently shared within the organization.

The process of identifying threat information sources includes the following steps:

- Identify sensors, tools, data feeds, and repositories that produce threat information, and confirm that the information is produced at a frequency, precision, and accuracy to support cybersecurity decision-making.

- Identify threat information that is collected and analyzed as part of an organization's continuous monitoring strategy.

- Locate threat information that is collected and stored, but not necessarily analyzed or reviewed on an ongoing basis. If an organization finds useful threat information that is being underutilized, methods of integrating this information into its cybersecurity and risk management practices should be explored.

- Identify threat information that is suitable for sharing with outside parties and that could help them more effectively respond to threats.

The owners and operators of threat information sources play an important role in the inventory process and should be consulted. These personnel understand what information is available and how it is natively stored; the data export formats that are supported; and the query languages, protocols, and services available for data retrieval. Some sources may store and publish structured, machine-readable data, while others may provide unstructured data with no fixed format (e.g., free text or images). Structured data that is expressed using open, machine-readable, standard formats can generally be more readily accessed, searched, and analyzed by a wider range of tools. Thus, the format of the information plays a significant role in determining the ease and efficiency of information use, analysis, and exchange.

As part of the inventory process, organizations should take note of information gaps that may prevent realization of the organization's goals and objectives. By identifying these gaps, an organization is better able to prioritize investments into new capabilities, and identify opportunities to fill gaps by acquiring threat information from other, possibly external, sources or through the deployment of additional tools or sensors.

Table 3-1 describes common sources of cybersecurity-related information and provides examples of data elements from these sources that may be of interest to security operations personnel.

Table 3-1: Selected Internal Information Sources

Source	Examples
Network Data Sources	
Router, firewall, Wi-Fi, remote services (such as remote login or remote command execution), and Dynamic Host Configuration Protocol (DHCP) server logs	Timestamp Source and destination IP address Domain name TCP/UDP port number Media Access Control (MAC) address Hostname Action (deny/allow) Status code Other protocol information

Source	Examples
Diagnostic and monitoring tools (network intrusion detection and prevention system, packet capture & protocol analysis)	Timestamp IP address, port, and other protocol information Network flow data Packet payload Application-specific information Type of attack (e.g., SQL injection, buffer overflow) Targeted vulnerability Attack status (success/fail/blocked)
Host Data Sources	
Operating system and application configuration settings, states, and logs	Bound and established network connection and port Process and thread Registry setting Configuration file entry Software version and patch level information Hardware information User and group File attribute (e.g., name, hash value, permissions, timestamp, size) File access System event (e.g., startup, shutdown, failures) Command history
Antivirus products	Hostname IP address MAC address Malware name Malware type (e.g., virus, hacking tool, spyware, remote access) File name File location (i.e., path) File hash Action taken (e.g., quarantine, clean, rename, delete)
Web browsers	Browser history and cache including: • Site visited • Object downloaded • Object uploaded • Browser extension installed or enabled • Cookies
Other Data Sources	
Security Information and Event Management (SIEM)	Summary reports synthesized from a variety of data sources (e.g., operating system, application, and network logs)
Email systems	Email messages: Email header content • Sender/recipient email address • Subject line • Routing information Attachments URLs Embedded graphic

Source	Examples
Help desk ticketing systems, incident management/tracking system, and people from within the organization	Analysis reports and observations regarding: • TTPs • Campaigns • Affiliations • Motives • Exploit code and tools • Response and mitigation strategies • Recommended courses of action User screen captures (e.g., error messages or dialog boxes)
Forensic toolkits and dynamic and/or virtual execution environments	Malware samples System artifacts (network, file system, memory)

Organizations should update the inventory when new sensors, repositories, or capabilities are deployed or when significant changes to a device's configuration, ownership, or administrative point of contact occur.

3.3 Define the Scope of Information Sharing Activities

Organizations should specify the scope of their information sharing activities by identifying the types of information available to share, the circumstances under which sharing this information is permitted, and those with whom the information can and should be shared. Organizations should review their information sharing goals and objectives while scoping information sharing activities to ensure that priorities are addressed. When defining these activities, organizations should ensure that the information sources and capabilities needed to support each activity are available. Organizations should also consider pursuing sharing activities that will address known information gaps. For example, an organization might not have an internal malware analysis capability, but it may gain access to malware indicators by participating in a sharing community.

The breadth of information sharing activities will vary based on an organization's resources and abilities. By choosing a relatively narrow scope, an organization with limited resources can focus on a smaller set of activities that provides the greatest value to the organization and its sharing partners. An organization may be able to expand the scope as additional capabilities and resources become available. Such an incremental approach may help to ensure that information sharing activities support an organization's information sharing goals and objectives, while at the same time fit within available resources. Organizations with greater resources and advanced capabilities may choose a larger initial scope that allows for a broader set of activities in support of their goals and objectives.

The degree of automation available to support the sharing and receipt of threat information is a factor to consider when establishing the scope of sharing activities. Less automated approaches or manual approaches, which require direct human intervention, may increase human resource costs and limit the breadth and volume of information that can be processed. The use of automated exchange mechanisms can help reduce human resource costs, and allow an organization to exchange threat information on a larger scale. Automated threat information sharing concepts are further discussed in section 4.

3.4 Establish Information Sharing Rules

Before sharing threat information, organizations should:

• List the types of threat information that may be shared.

- Describe the conditions and circumstances when sharing is permitted.

- Identify approved recipients of threat information.

- Describe any requirements for redacting or sanitizing information to be shared.

- Specify if source attribution is permitted.

- Apply information handling designations that describe recipient obligations for protecting information.

Sharing rules help control the publication and distribution of threat information, and consequently help to prevent the dissemination of information that, if improperly disclosed, may have adverse consequences for the organization or its customers or business partners. Information sharing rules should take into consideration the trustworthiness of the recipient, the sensitivity of the shared information, and the potential impacts of sharing (or not sharing). For example, an organization may establish rules that limit the exchange of highly sensitive information to internal individuals or groups, that allow the sharing of moderately sensitive information with specific trusted partners, that permit information having a low sensitivity to be published within a closed sharing community, and that allow for the free exchange of non-sensitive information within public information sharing forums.

Large organizations that want to share internal threat information across business units may also need to establish rules governing the exchange of threat information between organizational elements. Business units within an organization that either collect or process threat information should participate in scoping what types of threat information will be shared and how that will be done. The steps for establishing information sharing rules apply to internal sharing of threat information within large organizations. Multinational corporations need to consider the differences in various nation's privacy laws and how to address handling of classified information, which typically cannot be shared with foreign nationals.

When establishing and reviewing information sharing rules, organizations should request input from their legal and privacy officials, information owners, the management team, and other key stakeholders to ensure that the sharing rules align with the organization's documented policies and procedures. Sharing rules can specified in a variety of ways including, Memoranda of Understanding (MOUs), Non-Disclosure Agreements (NDAs), Framework Agreements[5], or other agreements. Organizations are encouraged to proactively establish threat information sharing agreements as part of their ongoing cybersecurity operations rather than attempting to put such agreements into place while under duress in the midst of an active cyber incident.

An organization's information sharing rules should be reevaluated on a regular basis. Some of the events that can trigger reevaluation are:

- Changes to regulatory or legal requirements,

- Updates to organizational policy,

- Introduction of new information sources,

- Risk tolerance changes,

---

[5] An example of such an agreement is the Defense Industrial Base (DIB) Cyber Security/Information Assurance (CS/IA) Program standardized Framework Agreement [4] which implements the requirements set forth in Title 32 Code of Federal Regulations, Part 236, Sections 236.4 through 236.6.

- Information ownership changes,

- Changes in the operating/threat environment, and

- Organizational mergers and acquisitions.

3.4.1   Information Sensitivity and Privacy

Many organizations handle information that, by regulation, law, or contractual obligation, requires protection. This includes PII, CUI, and other sensitive information afforded protection under the Sarbanes-Oxley Act (SOX), the Payment Card Industry Data Security Standard (PCI DSS), the Health Information Portability and Accountability Act (HIPAA), the Federal Information Security Modernization Act of 2014 (FISMA), and the Gramm-Leach-Bliley Act (GLBA) and other legislation, regulations, and guidelines. Organizations should identify and properly protect such information. An organization's legal team, privacy officers, auditors, and experts familiar with the various regulatory frameworks should be consulted when developing procedures for identifying and protecting sensitive information.

From a privacy perspective, one of the key challenges with threat information sharing is the potential for disclosure of PII[6]. Education and awareness activities are critical to ensure that individuals responsible for handling threat information understand how to recognize and safeguard PII.[7] Internal sharing of information may result in disclosure of PII to people who, by virtue of their job functions, would not typically have routine access to such information. For example, a forensic analyst or incident responder may encounter PII while searching a hard drive for malware indicators, reviewing emails related to suspected phishing attacks, or inspecting packet captures. The analyst has a legitimate need to review this information to investigate an exploit, develop detection strategies, or develop defensive measures. If the result of such an analysis is shared with others, steps should be taken to protect the confidentiality of PII.

An organization should have information sharing policies and procedures in place that provide guidance for the handling of PII. These policies and procedures should include steps for identifying incident data types that are likely to contain PII. Policies should describe proper safeguards for managing the privacy risks associated with sharing such data. A common practice is to focus on the exchange of indicators to the maximum extent possible. Some indicators, such as file hashes, network port numbers, registry key values, and other data elements, are largely free of PII. Where PII is identified, however, organizations should redact fields containing PII that are not relevant to investigating or addressing threats before sharing.[8] The type and degree of protection applied should be based on the intended use of the information, the sensitivity of the information, and the intended recipient.

---

[6] OMB Memorandum 07-16 [5] defines PII as "information which can be used to distinguish or trace an individual's identity, such as their name, social security number, biometric records, etc. alone, or when combined with other personal or identifying information which is linked or linkable to a specific individual, such as date and place of birth, mother's maiden name, etc." OMB Memorandum 10-22 [6] further states that "the definition of PII is not anchored to any single category of information or technology. Rather, it demands a case-by-case assessment of the specific risk that an individual can be identified. In performing this assessment, it is important for an agency to recognize that non-PII can become PII whenever additional information is made publicly available — in any medium and from any source — that, when combined with other available information, could be used to identify an individual." NIST SP 800-122 [7] includes a slightly different definition of PII that is focused on the security objective of confidentiality and not privacy in the broad sense. Definitions of PII established by organizations outside of the federal government may vary based on the consideration of additional regulatory requirements. The guidance in this document applies regardless of how organizations define PII.
[7] For additional guidance and examples of privacy controls, see NIST SP 800-53 Rev. 4, Appendix J, "Privacy Control Catalog, Privacy Controls, Enhancements, and Supplemental Guidance" [8].
[8] NIST SP 800-122 [7] describes a process called "de-identification" which entails the removal or obfuscation of PII, such that the remaining information cannot be used to identify an individual.

Where practical, organizations are encouraged to use automated methods rather than human-oriented methods to identify and protect PII. Manual identification, extraction, and obfuscation of PII can be a slow, error-prone, and resource-intensive process. Automated methods may include field-level data validation using permitted values lists, searching for PII using pattern matching techniques such as regular expressions, and performing operations that de-identify, mask, and anonymize data containing PII. The degree of automation that can be achieved will vary based on factors such as the structure, complexity, and sensitivity of the information.

Organizations should also implement safeguards to protect intellectual property, trade secrets, and other proprietary information from unauthorized disclosure. The disclosure of such information could result in financial loss, violate NDAs or other sharing agreements, be cause for legal action, or damage an organization's reputation. Organizations should have a plan in place to address the unauthorized or inadvertent disclosure of CUI. The plan should cover containment, control, and recovery procedures; breach notification requirements, and post-incident activities such as capturing lessons learned.

Table 3-2 introduces selected types of threat information, provides examples of sensitive data that may be present in these types of threat information, and offers general recommendations for handling such data.

Table 3-2: Handling Recommendations for Selected Types of Sensitive Data

Type of Threat Information	Examples of Sensitive Data Elements[9]	Recommendations
Network Indicators	Any single network indicator can be sensitive, but network indicators in the aggregate are often more sensitive because they can reveal relationships between network entities. By studying these relationships it may be possible to infer the identity of users, gather information about the posture of devices, perform network reconnaissance, and characterize the security safeguards and tools that an organization uses.	Focus on the exchange of network indicators such as destination IP addresses associated with an actor's command and control infrastructure, malicious URLs/domains, and staging servers. Before sharing, anonymize or sanitize network indicators that contain IP or MAC addresses of target systems or addresses registered to your organization. Also anonymize or sanitize indicators that may reveal the structure of internal networks, or ports or protocols that identify particular products.

---

[9] The PII confidentiality impact level as discussed in NIST SP 800-122 [7] is a useful tool for gauging sensitivity of PII.

Type of Threat Information	Examples of Sensitive Data Elements[9]	Recommendations
Packet Capture (PCAP)	In addition to the network indicators previously discussed, unencrypted or decrypted packets may contain authentication credentials and sensitive organization information, such as PII, CUI or other types of sensitive information.	PCAP files can be challenging because network indicators may be present within both the packet header and the payload. For example, PCAP files may show protocols (e.g., DHCP, Address Resolution Protocol (ARP), File Transfer Protocol (FTP), DNS) and applications operating at multiple layers within the network stack. These protocols and applications generate network information that may be captured within PCAP files and may require sanitization or anonymization to prevent sensitive information leakage. Filter PCAP files before sharing by extracting only those packets that are related to the investigation of a specific incident or pattern of events: • Related to a particular network conversation (i.e., exchange of information between specific IP addresses of interest); • Occurring during a chosen time period; • Destined for, or originating from, a specific port; or • Use of a particular network protocol. Redact payload content that contains PII, CUI or other types of sensitive information that is not relevant for characterizing the incident or event of interest. When anonymizing or redacting network information, use a strategy that preserves enough information to support meaningful analysis of the resulting PCAP file contents.
Network Flow Data	Network flow data contains information such as: • Source IP address (i.e., the sender), • Destination IP address (i.e., the recipient), • Port and protocol information, • Byte counts, and • Timestamps. If not effectively anonymized, network flow data may make identification of specific users possible, provide insights into user behavior (e.g., web sites visited), expose application and service usage patterns, or reveal network routing information and data volumes.	Before sharing network flow data, organizations should consider redacting portions of session histories using cryptography-based, prefix-preserving, IP address anonymization techniques to prevent network identification or to conceal specific fields within the session trace (e.g., time stamps, ports, protocols, or byte counts). To gain the greatest value from the information, use a tool that transforms network flow data without breaking referential integrity. Network flow analysis and correlation operations often require that IP address replacement and transformation operations are performed consistently within and sometimes across multiple files. Anonymization techniques that do not use a consistent replacement strategy may reduce or eliminate the value of sharing this type of information.

Type of Threat Information	Examples of Sensitive Data Elements[9]	Recommendations
Phishing Email Samples	Email headers may contain information such as: • Mail agent IP addresses, • Host or domain names, and • Email addresses. An email message body may also contain PII, CUI, or other types of sensitive information.	Organizations should anonymize email samples and remove any sensitive information that is not necessary for describing an incident or event of interest.
System, Network, and Application Logs	Log files may contain PII, CUI or other types of sensitive information. Log data may reveal IP addresses, ports, protocols, services, and URLs, as well as connection strings, logon credentials, portions of financial transactions, or other activities captured in URL parameters.	Organizations should perform IP address, timestamp, port, and protocol anonymization and remove any sensitive information that is not necessary for describing an incident or event of interest. Before sharing log data, it may also be necessary to sanitize URLs that contain identifying information such as session or user identifiers. Application logs may require redaction and anonymizing operations that are specific to particular application log formats.
Malware Indicators and Samples	Although organizations are unlikely to encounter sensitive information in malware indicators or samples, sensitive information may be present depending on how targeted the malware is and what collection methods were used to gather a sample.	Organizations should remove PII, CUI, and other types of sensitive information that is not necessary for describing an incident or event of interest.

3.4.2 Sharing Designations

A variety of methods exist to designate handling requirements for shared threat information. These designations identify unclassified information that may not be suitable for public release and that may require special handling. A designation applied to threat information can communicate specific handling requirements and identify data elements that are considered sensitive and should be redacted prior to sharing. Organizations are encouraged to provide clear handling guidance for any shared threat information. Likewise, recipients of threat information should observe the handling, attribution, dissemination, and storage requirements expressed in the source organization's handling guidance.

The Traffic Light Protocol (TLP), depicted in Table 3-3, provides a framework for expressing sharing designations [9].

Table 3-3: Traffic Light Protocol, Version 1.0

Color	When should it be used?	How may it be shared?
TLP:RED Not for disclosure, restricted to participants only.	Sources may use TLP:RED when information cannot be effectively acted upon by additional parties, and could lead to impacts on a party's privacy, reputation, or operations if misused.	Recipients may not share TLP:RED information with any parties outside of the specific exchange, meeting, or conversation in which it was originally disclosed. In the context of a meeting, for example, TLP:RED information is limited to those present at the meeting. In most circumstances, TLP:RED should be exchanged verbally or in person.
TLP:AMBER Limited disclosure, restricted to participants' organizations.	Sources may use TLP:AMBER when information requires support to be effectively acted upon, yet carries risks to privacy, reputation, or operations if shared outside of the organizations involved.	Recipients may only share TLP:AMBER information with members of their own organization, and with clients or customers who need to know the information to protect themselves or prevent further harm. Sources are at liberty to specify additional intended limits of the sharing: these must be adhered to.
TLP:GREEN Limited disclosure, restricted to the community.	Sources may use TLP:GREEN when information is useful for the awareness of all participating organizations as well as with peers within the broader community or sector.	Recipients may share TLP:GREEN information with peers and partner organizations within their sector or community, but not via publicly accessible channels. Information in this category can be circulated widely within a particular community. TLP:GREEN information may not be released outside of the community.
TLP:WHITE Disclosure is not limited.	Sources may use TLP:WHITE when information carries minimal or no foreseeable risk of misuse, in accordance with applicable rules and procedures for public release. Subject to standard copyright rules.	TLP:WHITE information may be distributed without restriction.

The TLP specifies a color-coded set of restrictions that indicate which restrictions apply to a particular record. In the TLP, red specifies the most restrictive rule, with information sharable only in a particular exchange or meeting, not even within a participant's own organization. The amber, green, and white color codes specify successively relaxed restrictions.

The Anti-Phishing Working Group (APWG) has also proposed a schema for expressing sharing designations [10]. The APWG schema describes an extensible, hierarchical tagging system that can be used to express distribution restrictions on shared information. The tags can be used to indicate with whom the information may or may not be shared (e.g., recipient only, with affected parties only, no restrictions) and to express other caveats (e.g., that no attribution is permitted).

For some threat information, collection methods may be considered confidential or proprietary, but the actual indicators observed may be shareable. In such cases, an organization may want to use *tear line reporting*, an approach where reports are organized such that information of differing sensitivity is not intermingled (e.g., the indicator information is presented in a separate part of the document than the collection methods). Organizing a report in this manner allows an organization to readily produce a report containing only information that designated recipients are authorized to receive.

An organization should carefully choose, or formulate, an approach for expressing sharing designations. Regardless of how an organization expresses sharing designations, the procedures for applying designations to threat information should be documented and approved, and the personnel responsible for assigning such designations properly trained.

3.4.3 Cyber Threat Information Sharing and Tracking Procedures

Over time, an organization's cybersecurity activities can result in the accumulation of large quantities of threat information from various sources, both internal and external. Though challenging, tracking of data sources is important both for protecting information owners and for ensuring that consuming organizations can meet their legal or regulatory commitments for data protection. Organizations should also preserve the provenance of data by tracking who provided the information and how the information was collected, transformed, or processed, information that is important for drawing conclusions from shared information.

An organization should formulate procedures that allow prompt sharing of threat information while at the same time satisfying its obligations for protecting potentially sensitive data. The procedures should, to the extent possible, balance the risks of possibly ineffective sharing against the risks of possibly flawed protection. An organization's information sharing and tracking procedures should:

- Identify threat information that can be readily shared with trusted parties.
- Establish processes for reviewing, sanitizing, and protecting threat information that is likely to contain sensitive information.
- Develop plan for addressing leakage of sensitive data.
- Automate the processing and exchange of threat information where possible.
- Describe how information handling designations are applied, monitored, and enforced.
- Accommodate non-attributed information exchange, when needed.
- Track internal and external sources of threat information.

The procedures should describe the roles, responsibilities, and authorities (both scope and duration) of all stakeholders. The procedures should allow for the effective transfer of authority and flow of shared information to key decision makers and should enable collaboration with approved external communities when needed.

3.5 Join a Sharing Community

When evaluating potential sharing partners, an organization should look to sources that complement its existing threat information resources or that offer actionable information that addresses known gaps in an organization's situational awareness. Since sharing communities may focus on the exchange of a specific type of threat information, an organization may need to participate in multiple information sharing forums to meet its information sharing objectives.

Threat information can be acquired from public and private sharing communities, government repositories, across the organization, commercial threat information feeds, and open sources. Sharing communities often organize around a shared characteristic or interest. The composition of a community may be based on geographic region, political boundary, industrial sector, business interest, or threat space (e.g., focused on phishing attacks). Many of these communities have multinational constituencies and global reach. Examples of potential sharing partners are ISACs, domestic and foreign Computer Emergency Readiness Teams (CERTs) or CSIRTs, Information Sharing and Analysis Organizations (ISAOs), DHS Automated Indicator Sharing (AIS) initiative, threat and vulnerability repositories, law enforcement agencies, product vendors, managed security service providers, internet service providers, supply chain partners, industry sector peers, business partners, and customers.

Some communities are informal, open, self-organizing groups that largely operate through voluntary cooperation. The membership of these communities is often mutable (i.e., no formal fixed membership), sometimes anonymous, and the members may maintain full autonomy with minimal central coordination. These communities generally operate under basic rules of conduct rather than formal agreements. In such communities, members publish threat information to the community on a voluntary, ad hoc basis and are individually responsible for ensuring that the content provided to the community is suitable for sharing. Organizations wishing to consume information can subscribe to or access various delivery mechanisms offered by a community such as web services, email or text alerts, and RSS feeds. Such sharing communities generally make no assertions regarding the quality and accuracy of data provided by their members, and the degree to which the information should be trusted depends on the reputation of submitters (if known).

In contrast, formal sharing communities may define specific membership rules such as:

- Membership fee structures;

- Eligibility requirements for institutions (e.g., must operate within a specific industry sector);

- Eligibility requirements for individuals (e.g., must have enterprise-wide security responsibilities);

- Nomination or sponsorship requirements (i.e., brokered trust);

- Probationary membership period requirements;

- Types of threat information the community provides/accepts;

- Standard delivery mechanisms, formats, and protocols supported by the community; and

- Required organizational cybersecurity capabilities.

Formal communities may recruit members by invitation or through sponsorship, and, as such, members are vetted. Membership rosters in formal communities are generally more stable than those of informal communities. The exchange of information in a formal community is often governed through service level agreements (SLAs), NDAs, and other agreements that describe the responsibilities of its members and participating organizations. Some communities collect an annual membership fee to cover the services and administrative costs of the community. These fees vary by community and the fee structure is sometimes tiered, providing for different levels of membership and service.

Before entering into information sharing agreements, an organization should obtain approval from the:

- Leadership team that has oversight for information sharing activities and for controlling the resources necessary to support the organization's information sharing goals;

- Legal team or those with the authority to enter into commitments; and

- Privacy officers and other key stakeholders that have a role in the collection, ingest, storage, analysis, publication, or protection of threat information.

When choosing a sharing community, consideration should be given to the types of information that are shared within the community, the structure and dynamics of the community, and the cost of entry and sustainment of membership. When evaluating how information is shared within a community, an organization should consider the following questions:

- Is the threat information shared within the community relevant and does it complement existing threat information by providing meaningful insights in the context of an organization's threat environment?

- Is the threat information exchanged within the community actionable?

- Does the community have mechanisms in place to accept non-attributed threat information submissions and the ability to protect a submitter's identity?

- Is the threat information timely, reliable, and of known good quality?

- Are the information exchange formats used by the community compatible with the infrastructure and tools used in an organization?

- Given the frequency and volume of data sent by a community, does an organization have the capacity to ingest/analyze/store the information?

In addition to the information shared within a community, consideration should also be given to the dynamics of the community and its participants, including:

- What is the size and composition of the community? (e.g., number of participants, information producers, and information consumers)

- How active is the community? (e.g., number of submissions or requests per day)

- Are community members recruited and vetted? If so, how?

- What are the technical skills and proficiencies of the community members?

- What is the community's governance model?

- What are the initial and sustained costs of membership?

- What type of sharing agreement does the community use?

- Is the sharing agreement well-aligned with an organization's goals, objectives, and business rules?

- What are the community's data retention and disposal policies?

When researching sharing communities, organizations are encouraged to have conversations with current or former members regarding their experiences as a participant in a community. Such conversation can provide additional insight and help an organization assess the trustworthiness of a prospective community.

3.6   Plan to Provide Ongoing Support for Information Sharing Activities

Organizations should develop a support plan that addresses information sharing infrastructure maintenance and user support. The plan should identify the personnel, funding, infrastructure, and processes needed to:

- Collect and analyze the information from both internal and external sources,

- Acquire and deploy protective measures, and

- Acquire and deploy a monitoring and threat detection infrastructure.

Organizations should provide funding for the personnel, infrastructure, and training required for ongoing operational support for data collection, storage, analysis, and dissemination; for technology refreshment; and for membership or service fees required for community participation. Although participation in information sharing activities will require ongoing funding, effective use of threat information may avoid the potentially much larger costs of successful attacks.

4.   Participating in Sharing Relationships

An organization's participation in an information sharing community will typically include some or all of the following activities:

- Engage in ongoing communication (section 4.1),

- Consume and respond to security alerts (section 4.2),

- Consume and use indicators (section 4.3),

- Organize and store indicators (section 4.4), and

- Produce and publish indicators (section 4.5).

The following sections describe these activities in greater detail. Organizations just starting their threat information sharing efforts should initially choose one or two activities to focus on and should consider adding activities as their information sharing capability matures. Organizations should understand that threat information sharing *augments*—not replaces—an organization's fundamental cybersecurity capabilities, regardless of the maturity of their information sharing practices.

4.1   Engage in Ongoing Communication

Information sharing communities use a variety of communications methods to share threat information with their members. Most organizations can receive threat information via email lists, text alerts, and web portals without infrastructure investments specific to information sharing, although the content received through these delivery channels may need to be manually processed (e.g., "cut and paste" into tools). Organizations with security tools that support standard data formats can use standards-based data feeds that enable semi-automated ingest, processing, and use of threat information. Other information sharing methods, such as conferences and workshops, require dedicated staff and travel. Organizations that actively produce and share threat information are likely to incur higher communication costs. Communications may be event-driven (i.e., in response to the actions or behavior of an actor) or periodic, such as bi-weekly reviews, teleconferences, and annual conferences.

The level of detail, volume, and frequency of messages delivered in human-readable formats varies widely across information sharing communities. Some communities seek to deliver the most current threat information with minimal latency. In contrast, some recipients using threat information for trending and analysis may prefer summary data and may have no need for near real-time delivery of detailed information. To reduce the number of messages generated, sharing communities sometimes provide the option of subscribing to digests (i.e., compilations of messages over time intervals) rather than receiving individual messages.

An organization that has recently joined an information sharing community may require time to integrate new threat information sources into its existing cybersecurity practices, configure security tools, and train decision makers on how to interpret and act upon the threat information. During this ramp-up period, an organization should consult any best practices guidance offered by a community, observe and learn from the interactions of more experienced members, and query community support resources (e.g., community knowledgebase, FAQs, blogs). Community-sponsored training events also provide opportunities for less mature organizations and inexperienced employees to gain practical insights from skilled practitioners. Organizations should also establish recruitment and retention processes that reduce personnel turnover and foster the formation of trusted professional relationships between sharing communities and organizations. Retention of skilled staff mitigates the loss of institutional knowledge, and preserves investments in training.

Ongoing participation in a sharing community is essential for fostering trust, establishing stronger ties to other members, and continuously improving practices. Organizations that actively participate in community-sponsored conference calls and face-to-face meetings are better able to establish trust with other members and consequently to effectively collaborate over time.

4.2   Consume and Respond to Security Alerts

An information sharing community may publish security alerts notifying community members of emerging vulnerabilities, exploits, and other security issues. Fields that commonly appear in security alerts such as US-CERT alerts, NVD vulnerability advisories, and vendor security bulletins include[10]:

- Brief overview/executive summary and detailed description, which would include indicators;

- Platforms affected (e.g., operating system, application, hardware);

- Estimated impact (e.g., system crash, data exfiltration, application hijacking)[11];

- Severity rating (e.g., Common Vulnerability Scoring System (CVSS) [11]);

- Mitigation options, including permanent fixes and/or temporary workarounds;

- References for more information; and

- Alert metadata (e.g., alert creation and modification dates, acknowledgments).

Upon receipt of a security alert, an organization should determine if the alert came from a trusted, reliable source. When alerts originate from unknown or untrusted sources, organizations may need to apply greater scrutiny and/or seek independent confirmation before taking action. If an alert is deemed credible and it applies to systems, applications, or hardware that the organization owns or operates; the organization should determine a suitable course of action.

When determining a proper response, an organization should characterize the overall impact of an alert by assessing factors such as the severity of the alert, the number of affected systems within the organization, the effects an attack might have on the organization's mission-critical functions, and any operational impacts related to the deployment of mitigating security controls. This assessment should inform the prioritization and approach for response actions. Response actions include activities such as identifying and extracting indicators from an alert, using indicators to develop and deploy detection signatures, making configuration changes, applying patches, notifying personnel of threats, and implementing or enhancing security controls. Extracting indicators is largely a manual process today but there are clear incentives for automating indicator handling workflows. Manual processing of indicators can be time-consuming, tedious, error-prone, and slow; automation of the activities allows analysts to focus on the interpretation of information, rather than routine data manipulations.

4.3   Consume and Use Indicators

The consumption and use of indicators from external feeds is often a multi-step process that includes some, if not all, of the following activities:

---

[10] Source: US-CERT (https://www.us-cert.gov/).

[11] A more extensive list of potential effects is given in the MITRE Common Weakness Enumeration (http://cwe.mitre.org/) and Common Vulnerabilities and Exposures (http://cve.mitre.org/) listings.

- **Validation:** verifying the integrity of indicator content and provenance through digital signatures, cryptographic hashes, or other means.

- **Decryption:** transforming encrypted indicator files or data streams back to their original format.

- **Decompression:** unpacking compressed indicator files, archive files (e.g., zip, tar), or data streams.

- **Content extraction:** parsing indicator files and extracting indicators of interest to an organization.[12]

- **Prioritization:** processing indicators based on relative importance, the perceived value of a data source, the overall confidence in the data, any operational requirements that specify that data sources be processed in a particular order, the amount of effort required to transform the data into actionable information, or other factors.

- **Categorization:** reviewing indicator metadata to determine its security designation and handling requirements. Sensitive information may require encrypted storage, more stringent access control, or limitations on distribution.

These activities are typically performed in the order described above, but the order may vary based on specific operational or security requirements. Where feasible, organizations are encouraged to use automated techniques to make the indicators available more quickly and reduce manual effort. In cases where indicators are being informally shared, such as through email, indicator prioritization and categorization are still important and should be performed by the recipient.

Ideally, indicators are:

- **Timely.** Indicators should be delivered with minimal latency thereby allowing additional time for recipients to prepare suitable responses. The time criticality of indicators depends on the characteristics of the threats, including their severity, speed, and ease of propagation, the infrastructure being targeted, the TTPs being used, and the capabilities of the actor(s).

- **Relevant.** Indicators should be applicable to a recipient's operating environment and address threats the organization is likely to face. The unnecessary processing of extraneous indicators creates additional work for analysts and slows down prioritization and categorization actions.

- **Accurate.** Indicators should be correct, complete, and unambiguous. Inaccurate or incomplete information introduces uncertainty and may prevent critical action, stimulate unnecessary action, result in ineffective responses, or instill a false sense of security. Recipients should be made aware of any uncertainty or caveats regarding the accuracy of an indicator.

- **Specific.** Indicators should provide clear descriptions of observable events that recipients can use to detect threats while minimizing false positives/negatives.

- **Actionable.** Indicators should provide enough information and context to allow recipients to develop a suitable response.

In practice, an indicator may exhibit some, but not all, of these characteristics. For example, a lone indicator may be ambiguous, but when aggregated and analyzed with threat information from other

---

[12] The extraction and handling of content like malware samples should be limited to organizations and individuals who have the knowledge, ability, and infrastructure needed to safely analyze malware. Special handling precautions should be stated and followed to prevent inadvertent introduction of malicious code onto production networks.

sources the indicator is enriched and demonstrates additional value. Also threat information from multiple sources may vary in precision and accuracy and it is important for users to be able to evaluate the information and assign tags that describe the quality or confidence level of the information. The tags are especially important when an organization needs to resolve discrepancies between threat information sources. As organizations enrich indicators, any new insights should be shared so that the entire community may benefit. Organizations may, for example, use externally and internally-generated indicators to:

- Add or modify rules or signatures used by firewalls, intrusion detection systems, data loss prevention systems, and/or other security controls to block or alert on activity matching the indicators (for example, connections involving IP addresses on a blacklist);

- Configure security information and event management solutions or other log management-related systems to help with analysis of security log data;

- Scan security logs, systems, or other sources of information, using indicators as search keys, to identify systems that may have already been compromised;

- Find matching records when investigating an incident or potential incident to learn more about a threat, and to help hasten incident response and recovery actions;

- Provide additional information to security operations center analysts;

- Educate staff on threat characteristics; and

- Identify threat trends that may suggest changes to security controls are needed.

Typically, an organization's willingness to use indicators from external sources is strongly affected by the level of trust the organization has in the source. Indicators received from a trusted source might be put to immediate use to detect and respond to a threat. In contrast, indicators originating from an untrusted source may require independent validation, additional research, or testing before use. Indicator use might also be affected by other factors, such as an organization's tolerance for service disruptions. For some organizations, security is paramount and occasionally blocking benign activity is considered acceptable. For other organizations, service availability may be so important that possible malicious activity might only trigger monitoring.

An organization should carefully consider the characteristics of indicators that it receives and should take a risk-based approach to determining how indicators can be most effectively used. An organization may find that a specific indicator is useful in some situations but not in others. Ultimately each organization must decide how to best use indicators.

4.4   Organize and Store Cyber Threat Information

Organizations may collect indicators from a variety of sources, including open source repositories, commercial threat feeds, and external partners. Depending on how indicators are being used, there may be a need to organize them in a knowledgebase. Free-form methods such as wikis can be quite flexible and suitable for developing working notes and indicator metadata. Structured databases are also useful for storing, organizing, tracking, querying, and analyzing collections of indicators.

Information commonly recorded in a knowledgebase includes the following, when known:

- Source of an indicator;

- Rules governing the use or sharing of an indicator;

- Date or time an indicator was collected;

- Length of time that an indicator is still considered valid;

- Whether or not attacks associated with an indicator have targeted specific organizations or sectors;

- Any Common Vulnerability Enumeration (CVE), Common Platform Enumeration (CPE), Common Weakness Enumeration (CWE), Common Configuration Enumeration (CCE) records associated with an indicator;

- Groups or actors associated with an indicator;

- Aliases of any associated actors;

- TTPs commonly used by an actor;

- Motives or intent of an associated actor;

- Individuals or types of individuals targeted in associated attacks; and

- Systems targeted in attacks.

An indicator knowledgebase is an attractive target of attack; therefore effective security practices should be followed, including implementing access controls, performing regular backups, maintaining operating system and application software by installing current patches, verifying secure configurations, and following software development best practices for the production of any in-house software used for the knowledgebase.[13]

Organizations should establish policies and procedures that address the disposition of indicators (and threat information in general). Policies and procedures should define data retention requirements for short (online) and long (offline) term availability of indicator information. Information handling and retention requirements may change once threat information is entered into evidence. Evidence acquired during any incident investigations, for instance, should be collected and preserved using best practices for data preservation following chain of custody requirements and other laws pertaining to the submission of evidence. A more detailed treatment of forensic techniques related to chain of custody and preserving information integrity is available in NIST Special Publication 800-86 [12] and Section 3.3.2 of NIST Special Publication 800-61 [1].

For indicators that are not needed as evidence, organizations should determine proper retention policies.[14] Although retaining threat information has costs, detailed information may provide historical value as well as help new sharing community members and partners understand the persistence and evolution of different actors and attack types. Other considerations, such as financial, legal, contractual, or regulatory issues, may limit data retention to a fixed period of months or years. Once a retention schedule is identified, organizations should either archive or destroy the indicators per applicable policies.[15]

---

[13] The NIST Software Assurance Metrics and Tool Evaluation (SAMATE) project seeks to develop standard evaluation measures and methods for software assurance. See http://samate.nist.gov/index.php/SAMATE_Publications.html.

[14] Federal agencies are subject to the National Archives and Records Administration (NARA) General Records Schedule as well as agency-specific retention policies.

[15] NIST SP 800-88 [14] provides guidance to assist organizations in making risk-based decisions regarding the sanitization and disposition of media and information.

4.5   Produce and Publish Indicators

Many organizations only consume indicators. However, some organizations, often those with more advanced security capabilities, choose to produce and publish their own indicators. An organization may benefit substantially by producing threat information. For example, an organization may gain greater expertise, help other organizations more effectively respond to threats in their environments, and foster trust with other community members. These effects are important for building and sustaining the flow of threat information that ultimately benefits a producing organization. A producer of shared threat information must decide what, if any, metadata should accompany shared information, what data formats should be used, how sensitive data should be handled, and how information sharing rules should be updated over time. The following subsections address these issues.

4.5.1   Indicator Enrichment

Indicators that are produced and published should include metadata that provides context for each indicator, describes how the indicator is to be used and interpreted and how the indicator relates to other indicators. Metadata may also include sensitivity designations and provenance information (e.g., what tool was used to acquire the data, how the data was processed, who collected the data). As indicators are created, aggregated, or enriched, their sensitivity and classification should be reevaluated. An aggregation, association, or enrichment process may enable re-identification (e.g., using data mining techniques) or elevate the sensitivity of the information, thus necessitating additional data handling restrictions.

The indicator production process should provide a mechanism for publishing indicators, updating indicators and associated metadata, and retracting submissions that are incorrect or perhaps inadvertently shared. Any automated mechanisms should be hardened and tested to ensure that they do not become viable attack vectors for threat actors. Organizations that share indicators should provide a feedback mechanism that allows sharing partners to submit error reports, suggest improvements, or request additional information about the indicators. Such feedback plays an important role in the enrichment, maturation, and quality of the indicators shared within a community.

Some information shared within a community may be marked as "currently under investigation" and may require that members avoid sharing beyond the collective; such markings may also prohibit members from performing active information collection (such as retrieving malware samples from a suspect website, or performing DNS lookups on suspect hostnames) that might tip off a potential actor or otherwise compromise investigative activities. At some point, such information will probably have its distribution and investigation restrictions downgraded, so a mechanism to change the marking or to add a revised marking such as "downgraded to GREEN as of 12/20/2015" is useful.

4.5.2   Standard Data Formats

The use of standard data formats for the exchange of indicators enhances interoperability and allows information to be exchanged with greater speed. Unstructured formats (e.g., text documents, email) are suitable for high-level threat reports and ad hoc exchanges of indicator information and other materials intended to be read by security personnel rather than machines. For time-critical exchanges of indicators, however, such as automatically configuring a firewall to block specified communications, the use of standard data formats is encouraged because such formats reduce the need for human assistance.

Organizations are encouraged to participate in threat information sharing standards development activities by sharing use cases, identifying desired features, and providing feedback to standards development organizations.[16] Organizations should seek out data formats and exchange protocols that can effectively support their key threat information sharing use cases, demonstrate a high degree of maturity, broad adoption, and enable interoperability between a wide range of products and/or organizations.

4.5.3 Protection of Sensitive Data

The indicators that an organization publishes may be sensitive, so proper safeguards should be used to prevent unauthorized disclosure or modification. Indicator data can be protected using a variety of methods, including encrypted network communications, authentication and authorization mechanisms, and storage in a hardened repository. If a repository is used, an organization should have a written SLA for the repository that specifies expected availability, security posture requirements, and acceptable use policies. When producing indicators that may contain sensitive information, proper sharing rules (see section 3.4) should be followed, and information should be shared only with community members that are trusted to follow sharing rules and that have agreed to do so.

---

[16] For example, cyber threat information sharing standards development activities have been conducted in both the Organization for the Advancement of Structured Information Standards (OASIS) and Internet Engineering Task Force (IETF) standards organizations.

This appendix presents some scenarios that describe threat information sharing in real-world applications. These scenarios seek to show how sharing and coordination can increase the efficiency and effectiveness of an organization's cybersecurity capabilities. These scenarios represent only a small number of the possible applications of information sharing and collaboration.

Scenario 1: Nation-State Attacks against a Specific Industry Sector

A nation-state regularly targets companies in a certain industry sector over several months. The attacks come in the form of targeted emails that carry malicious attachments containing a software exploit that, upon opening, launches malware on a victim's system. Systems that are successfully compromised by the malware are then reconfigured by the malware to contact command and control servers and other infrastructure operated by the actor to receive additional instructions, download other malware, and perform data exfiltration.

Many companies within this industry sector are members of a formal threat information sharing organization in which a central forum is used to post information about observed threats. The posts describe details relevant to detecting and defending against the threat, such as the sender addresses of phishing emails, samples of malware collected from the attacks, analysis of exploit code used by actors, the IPs and URLs associated with the actor's command and control servers, and other infrastructure involved with attacks.

As soon as one company's security team identifies a new attack, the information is shared with its peers within the forum. One of the companies (A) that participates in the forum has advanced malware analysis capabilities and is able to further characterize the actor and its command and control infrastructure using a malware sample shared via the forum by another company (B). Company A then shares back the information gained through its analysis of the malware. Through B's sharing of the malware sample, the community benefits from the malware analysis capabilities of company A, and is able to quickly and efficiently detect and protect against similar attacks. In this scenario, an attack faced by one company contributes to another's defense.

Scenario 2: Campaign Analysis

Cybersecurity analysts from companies in a business sector have been sharing indicators and malware samples in an online forum over the past few years. Each company performs independent analysis of the attacks and observes consistent patterns over time, with groups of events often having some commonalities, such as the type of malware used, the DNS domains of command and control channels, and other technical indicators. These observations lead the analysts to suspect that the attacks are not fully random, but part of a larger coordinated set of actions.

The forum members participate in technical exchange meetings to share data, insights, and analyses of the different attacks. Through data aggregation and joint analyses, the members can identify activities that are likely attributable to a common actor or to coordination among actors. This scenario demonstrates how data fusion and analysis may help reveal collective action and campaigns by a threat actor and identify the TTPs that are used by specific actors as part of a campaign.

Scenario 3: Distributed Denial of Service Attack against an Industry Sector

A hacktivist group targets a select set of companies for a large-scale distributed denial of service (DDoS) attack. The group uses a distributed botnet that is loosely coordinated and controlled by members of the group. By analyzing traffic generated by the botnet, one of the companies targeted in the attack is able to determine that the actors are using a variant of a popular DDoS tool.

The targeted companies are members of an ISAC and use the ISAC's discussion portal to establish a working group to coordinate incident response activities. The working group contacts the ISAC's law enforcement liaison, who coordinates with federal and international authorities to aid in the investigation and to gain court orders to shut down the actor's systems.

The working group contacts various internet service providers (ISPs), and provides information to aid in identifying abnormal traffic to their network addresses. The ISPs assist both the affected companies and law enforcement personnel by helping to identify the upstream and downstream traffic sources, implementing routing changes, and enforcing data rate limits on these sources. Using network traffic collected by the ISPs, law enforcement agencies can identify the command and control servers, seize these assets, and identify some members of the hacktivist group.

After a technical exchange meeting among the targeted companies, several companies decide to enlist the services of content distribution providers to deploy DDoS-resistant web architectures.

Scenario 4: Financial Conference Phishing Attack

A cyber crime group makes use of a publicly available conference attendee list to target specific individuals with a wave of phishing emails. The group is able to identify attendees who are members of the target organization's corporate accounting team (i.e., individuals who may have the authority to authorize payments or funds transfers). Using targeted malware, distributed through phishing attacks, the group tries to compromise machines and accounts to complete unauthorized electronic payments and funds transfers to overseas businesses.

One company is able to identify the phishing attack against personnel within its corporate accounting team and learns, during their investigation, that all the recipients targeted during the attack had attended the same conference six months earlier. The company's CSIRT contacts the conference organizers, as well as representatives from other organizations that attended the conference. The affected organizations arrange a conference call to share specific information (e.g., email header content, attachments, embedded URLs) regarding the attacks. Using the shared indicators, other conference attendees review their mail and network traffic logs to identify potentially compromised hosts. These companies agree to ongoing collaboration and information sharing about future attacks via an informal email list.

Scenario 5: Business Partner Compromise

"Company A" and "Company B" are business partners that have established network connectivity between their organizations to enable the exchange of business information. A cyber crime organization compromises a server at Company B and uses that access as a stepping stone to launch attacks against internal servers at Company A. Operations personnel at Company A notice the unusual activity and notify their security team. The security team identifies the source of the activity as coming from a Company B system. As stipulated in their business partner connectivity agreement, Company A notifies Company B about the anomalous traffic and the companies initiate a joint response to the incident following established procedures. Company A's incident response team describes the activity that it sees, allowing Company B's team to isolate the compromised server and perform an investigation to identify the source of the breach and other possible compromises. Company B's investigation reveals that the actors exploited a software flaw in a web-facing application and used it to gain unauthorized access to the server. The application development team at Company B makes a code change and deploys a patch that fixes the vulnerability, and the security operations team deploys logging and intrusion detection signatures to identify any similar future attacks.

Because the security teams of the two companies had agreements and processes in place for a joint response, had pre-established contacts and existing trust relationships, and had already understood each other's networks and operations, the companies were able to quickly respond and recover from the incident.

Scenario 6: US-CERT Provides Indicators, Receives Feedback

The US-CERT receives information, from a variety of independent sources, that servers located in the U.S. are being used to carry out cyber attacks against other U.S. companies. A specific foreign actor is known to control the compromised servers. The US-CERT identifies the targeted companies and notes that most operate within the aviation industry. The US-CERT contacts the security teams of these companies and shares initial threat information, including URLs, malware, and vulnerabilities being exploited by the actor.

Using the indicators, some of the affected companies are able to detect attacks against their infrastructures and to take the actions necessary to prevent the attacks from being successful. While investigating incidents, the affected companies are also able to identify new indicators or provide context regarding the attack to the US-CERT. The US-CERT is able to share these new indicators with other firms after anonymizing the sources, which leads to a more comprehensive response to the threat.

Scenario 7: A Retailer Fails to Share

A large retailer is subject to a cyber attack by a criminal organization. Millions of credit card numbers and account information are stolen during a breach that goes undiscovered for several weeks. The retailer does not share threat information and relies on its own security and detection capabilities. The retailer's internal capabilities prove inadequate in the face of a sophisticated, targeted threat that uses custom malware.

The breach is discovered by credit card companies investigating a rash of credit card fraud. The credit card companies determine that the commonality in the credit card fraud was purchases made from this one retailer. The credit card companies notify both law enforcement and the retailer, and an investigation is initiated.

The damages are extensive. The retailer notifies its customers of the theft of personal information, but does not release details of how the attack was carried out. Consequently, several other retailers are successfully attacked using the same methods in the weeks following the initial breach. The financial losses realized by the retailers, customers, and credit card issuers and the reputation loss to the retailers could have been avoided, at least in part, had the retailers engaged in active sharing of threat information with one another. The attacker is emboldened by the successful attack and benefits from the delayed response and lack of a coordination. The attacker benefits financially from the fraudulent activity and can use these additional resources to expand the scope and sophistication of their operations.

Appendix B—Glossary

Selected terms used in the publication are defined below.

Actor	See *threat actor*.
Alert	A brief, usually human-readable, technical notification regarding current vulnerabilities, exploits, and other security issues. Also known as an advisory, bulletin, or vulnerability note.
Continuous Monitoring	Maintaining ongoing awareness of information security, vulnerabilities, and threats to support organizational risk management decisions. [15]
Controlled Unclassified Information	Information that law, regulation, or government-wide policy requires to have safeguarding or disseminating controls, excluding information that is classified under Executive Order 13526, *Classified National Security Information*, December 29, 2009, or any predecessor or successor order, or the Atomic Energy Act of 1954, as amended. [16]
Cyber Threat	See *threat*.
Indicator	A technical artifact or observable that suggests an attack is imminent or is currently underway, or that a compromise may have already occurred.
Information Sharing and Analysis Organization	An ISAO is any entity or collaboration created or employed by public- or private sector organizations, for purposes of gathering and analyzing critical cyber and related information in order to better understand security problems and interdependencies related to cyber systems, so as to ensure their availability, integrity, and reliability. [17]
Metadata	Information describing the characteristics of data including, for example, structural metadata describing data structures (e.g., data format, syntax, and semantics) and descriptive metadata describing data contents (e.g., information security labels). [8]
Observable	An event (benign or malicious) on a network or system.
Phishing	Tricking individuals into disclosing sensitive personal information through deceptive computer-based means. [19]
Rootkit	A set of tools used by an attacker after gaining root-level access to a host to conceal the attacker's activities on the host and permit the attacker to maintain root-level access to the host through covert means. [18]
Sensitive Information	Information, the loss, misuse, or unauthorized access to or modification of, that could adversely affect the national interest or the conduct of federal programs, or the privacy to which individuals are entitled under 5 U.S.C. Section 552a (the Privacy Act), but that has not been specifically authorized under criteria established by an Executive Order or an Act of Congress to be kept classified in the interest of national defense or foreign policy. [18]

Sensor	An intrusion detection and prevention system component that monitors and analyzes network activity and may also perform prevention actions. [14]
Tactics, Techniques, and Procedures (TTPs)	The behavior of an actor. A tactic is the highest-level description of this behavior, while techniques give a more detailed description of behavior in the context of a tactic, and procedures an even lower-level, highly detailed description in the context of a technique.
Threat	Any circumstance or event with the potential to adversely impact organizational operations (including mission, functions, image, or reputation), organizational assets, individuals, other organizations, or the Nation through an information system via unauthorized access, destruction, disclosure, or modification of information, and/or denial of service. [2]
Threat Actor	An individual or a group posing a threat.
Threat Information	Any information related to a threat that might help an organization protect itself against a threat or detect the activities of an actor. Major types of threat information include indicators, TTPs, security alerts, threat intelligence reports, and tool configurations.
Threat Intelligence	Threat information that has been aggregated, transformed, analyzed, interpreted, or enriched to provide the necessary context for decision-making processes.
Threat Intelligence Report	A prose document that describes TTPs, actors, types of systems and information being targeted, and other threat-related information.
Threat Shifting	The response of actors to perceived safeguards and/or countermeasures (i.e., security controls), in which actors change some characteristic of their intent/targeting in order to avoid and/or overcome those safeguards/countermeasures. [2]
Tool Configuration	A recommendation for setting up and using tools that support the automated collection, exchange, processing, analysis, and use of threat information.
Watering Hole Attack	A security exploit where the attacker infects websites that are frequently visited by members of the group being attacked, with a goal of infecting a computer used by one of the targeted group when they visit the infected website.

Appendix C—Acronyms

Selected acronyms used in the publication are defined below.

ACL	Access Control List
ARP	Address Resolution Protocol
CCE	Common Configuration Enumeration
CIO	Chief Information Officer
CISO	Chief Information Security Officer
CPE	Common Platform Enumeration
CSIRT	Computer Security Incident Response Team
CUI	Controlled Unclassified Information
CVE	Common Vulnerability Enumeration
CVSS	Common Vulnerability Scoring System
CWE	Common Weakness Enumeration
DDoS	Distributed Denial of Service
DHCP	Dynamic Host Configuration Protocol
DIB	Defense Industrial Base
DNS	Domain Name System
FISMA	Federal Information Security Modernization Act
FTP	File Transfer Protocol
GLBA	Gramm-Leach-Bliley Act
HIPAA	Health Information Portability and Accountability Act
IP	Internet Protocol
IR	Interagency Report or Internal Report
ISAC	Information Sharing and Analysis Center
ISAO	Information Sharing and Analysis Organization
ISP	Internet Service Provider
IT	Information Technology
ITL	Information Technology Laboratory
MAC	Media Access Control
MOU	Memorandum of Understanding
NDA	Non-Disclosure Agreement
NIST	National Institute of Standards and Technology
NVD	National Vulnerability Database
OMB	Office of Management and Budget
PCAP	Packet Capture
PCI DSS	Payment Card Industry Data Security Standard
PII	Personally Identifiable Information
PSIRT	Product Security Incident Response Team
RSS	Rich Site Summary or Really Simple Syndication
SIEM	Security Information and Event Management
SLA	Service Level Agreement
SOX	Sarbanes-Oxley Act
SP	Special Publication
SQL	Structured Query Language
TCP	Transmission Control Protocol
TLP	Traffic Light Protocol
TTP	Tactics, Techniques, and Procedures
UDP	User Datagram Protocol

URL	Uniform Resource Locator
US-CERT	United States Computer Emergency Readiness Team

Appendix D—References

[1]   NIST SP 800-61, Revision 2, *Computer Security Incident Handling Guide*, August 2012.
       http://dx.doi.org/10.6028/NIST.SP.800-61r2

[2]   NIST SP 800-30, Revision 1, *Guide for Conducting Risk Assessments*, September 2012.
       http://dx.doi.org/10.6028/NIST.SP.800-30r1

[3]   Executive Order 12968, *Access to Classified Information*, August 2, 1995.
       http://www.gpo.gov/fdsys/pkg/FR-1995-08-07/pdf/95-19654.pdf [accessed 9/30/2016]

[4]   Defense Industrial Base (DIB) Cyber Security/Information Assurance (CS/IA) Program
       standardized Framework Agreement, *Federal Register* 78 FR 64230, October 22, 2013.
       http://www.gpo.gov/fdsys/pkg/FR-2013-10-22/pdf/2013-24256.pdf [accessed 9/30/2016]

[5]   OMB Memorandum 07-16, *Safeguarding Against and Responding to the Breach of Personally
       Identifiable Information*, May 22, 2007.
       https://www.whitehouse.gov/sites/default/files/omb/memoranda/fy2007/m07-16.pdf [accessed
       9/30/2016]

[6]   OMB Memorandum 10-22, *Guidance for Online Use of Web Measurement and Customization
       Technology*, June 25, 2010.
       https://www.whitehouse.gov/sites/default/files/omb/assets/memoranda_2010/m10-22.pdf
       [accessed 9/30/2016]

[7]   NIST SP 800-122, *Guide to Protecting the Confidentiality of Personally Identifiable Information
       (PII)*, April 2010.
       http://dx.doi.org/10.6028/NIST.SP.800-122

[8]   NIST SP 800-53, Revision 4, *Security and Privacy Controls for Federal Information Systems and
       Organizations*, April 2013 (updated 01-22-2015). http://dx.doi.org/10.6028/NIST.SP.800-53r4

[9]   FIRST, *Traffic Light Protocol (TLP): FIRST Standards Definitions and Usage Guidance –
       Version 1.0*, September 2016.
       https://www.first.org/_assets/resources/tlp-v1.pdf [accessed 9/30/2016]

[10]   Anti-Phishing Working Group [Github project site],
       https://github.com/patcain/ecrisp/tree/master/schemas/apwg [accessed 9/30/2016]

[11]   NIST IR 7435, *The Common Vulnerability Scoring System (CVSS) and Its Applicability to Federal
       Agency Systems*, August 2007.
       http://dx.doi.org/10.6028/NIST.IR.7435

[12]   NIST SP 800-86, *Guide to Integrating Forensic Techniques into Incident Response*, August 2006.
       http://dx.doi.org/10.6028/NIST.SP.800-86

[13]   NIST SP 800-88 Revision 1, *Guidelines for Media Sanitization*, December 2014.
       http://dx.doi.org/10.6028/NIST.SP.800-88r1

[14]   NIST SP 800-94, *Guide to Intrusion Detection and Prevention Systems (IDPS)* February 2007.
       http://dx.doi.org/10.6028/NIST.SP.800-94

[15]   NIST SP 800-137, *Information Security Continuous Monitoring (ISCM) for Federal Information
       Systems and Organizations*, September 2011.
       http://dx.doi.org/10.6028/NIST.SP.800-137

[16]   NIST SP 800-171, *Protecting Controlled Unclassified Information in Nonfederal Information
       Systems and Organizations*, June 2015 (updated 01-14-2016).
       http://dx.doi.org/10.6028/NIST.SP.800-171

[17]   ISAO Standards Organization, *Information Sharing and Analysis Organization Standards Organization Product Outline v0.2*, May 2, 2016.
        https://www.isao.org/drafts/isao-so-product-outline-v0-2 [accessed 9/30/2016]

[18]   NIST IR 7298 Revision 2, *Glossary of Key Information Security Terms*, May 2013.
        http://dx.doi.org/10.6028/NIST.IR.7298r2

[19]   NIST SP 800-83 Revision 1, *Guide to Malware Incident Prevention and Handling for Desktops and Laptops*, July 2013.
        http://dx.doi.org/10.6028/NIST.SP.800-83r1